BUILDING CONSTRUCTION

BUILDING CONSTRUCTION
MELVIN BERGER

327679

INDUSTRY AT WORK
FRANKLIN WATTS · NEW YORK · LONDON · 1978

JOHNSON FREE PUBLIC LIBRARY
HACKENSACK, N. J.

Photographs courtesy of: Port Authority of New York and New Jersey/Belva: p. 2,/Sheehan: p. 29,/ D.B.: p. 43 (top); National Association of Home Builders: pp. 3 (top), 26 (top), 32 (bottom), 37 (top), 46, 60; American Iron and Steel Institute: p. 3 (bottom); Gil Amiaga, Michael Harris Spector and Associates: p. 5 (all); Kyle T. Hallsteen, George A. Fuller Company: pp. 6 (top), 13 (top), 16 (top and bottom), 18, 57; Worklife Magazine: pp. 6 (bottom), 8 (top and bottom), 23 (top), 43 (bottom); Manpower Magazine: p. 40 (bottom); Skidmore Owings and Merrill: p. 13 (bottom); Portland Cement Association: p. 23 (bottom); Department of Housing and Urban Development: p. 26 (bottom); Vocational Industrial Clubs of America: pp. 32 (top), 51, 52; Bureau of Cooperative Education, Nassau County, N.Y.: pp. 37 (bottom left), 40 (top); National Roofing Contractors Association: p. 37 (bottom right).

Cover photograph courtesy of: Vocational Industrial Clubs of America.

Library of Congress Cataloging in Publication Data

Berger, Melvin.
    Building construction.

    (Industry at work series)
    Bibliography: p.
    Includes index.
    SUMMARY: Describes various jobs in the construction industry including architect, surveyor, iron worker, roofer, stone mason, and landscaper.
    1. Building trades—Vocational guidance—Juvenile literature. [1. Building trades—Vocational guidance. 2. Vocational guidance] I. Title. II. Series.
TH149.B47   690'.023   78-6258
ISBN 0-531-02206-4

Copyright © 1978 by Melvin Berger
All rights reserved
Printed in the United States of America
6 5 4 3 2 1

CONTENTS

INTRODUCTION
1

THE PLANNERS
10

STRUCTURAL CRAFTS
20

FINISHING CRAFTS
35

MECHANICAL CRAFTS
48

FURTHER READING
62

INDEX
64

INTRODUCTION

Construction is the biggest industry in America. About 5 million men and women work in the construction industry. More than $130 billion is spent on new construction every year.

The greatest part of this industry is building construction. Each year builders put up over 1 million houses, from single-family private homes to huge multidwelling apartment complexes; thousands of public buildings are erected, from schools and hospitals to zoos; business buildings are constructed, from giant shopping centers to tiny ice cream stands; industrial buildings rise too, from long auto factories to open shed lumber mills; and, of course, high-rise buildings and skyscrapers are built.

The other part of the industry is concerned with heavy construction. Heavy construction includes all structures that are not classified as buildings, such as city streets and superhighways, train and auto tunnels, pipe-

Workers installing steel for the
104th floor of the World Trade Center.

Above: Every year builders construct over one million houses. Left: Heavy construction includes building bridges.

lines and powerlines, ball fields and parks, and almost all water-connected structures, such as dams, bridges, piers, and docks.

Construction methods, of course, differ from project to project. Some large construction projects involve hundreds of workers, each one doing a specialized task. Smaller jobs employ a few workers, each one taking care of several tasks. But whatever the size, every construction project involves four basic steps.

The first step is to plan the project. The planners in the construction industry are architects and engineers. They consider the following: what are the uses for the project? how much money is available? how can the project be made most attractive? what materials and methods would make it a safe, long-lasting structure?

Next, the plans go to a contractor, who is in charge of the actual construction. The contractor hires the carpenters, bricklayers, cement, concrete, and stone masons, ironworkers, operating engineers, and laborers. These people are the structural workers. They are skilled in the different building trades. They operate heavy equipment to dig the holes for the foundation. They erect the steel, concrete, and wood parts of the buildings. They install glass, lay bricks, and do much more. They carry out the basic, rough part of the architect's plan.

The finish workers follow on the heels of the structural workers. Among the finish workers are roofers, painters, plasterers, and tile and marble setters. They install the floor and the roof, erect the inside and outside

The steps in construction, from architect's drawing—to construction—to finished building.

Above: The planning is done by the architect and the engineer who design the building. Right: Construction workers actually put up the building.

walls, put tiles in the bathroom, and insulate and decorate where necessary. They put the final touches on the job.

Then, while the finish workers are still on the site, the mechanical workers arrive. These are the electricians, plumbers, elevator constructors, sheet metal workers, and heating and air-conditioning installers. They install the fixtures, such as sinks and toilets, the equipment, such as furnaces and air conditioners, and the machines, such as clothes washers and dryers.

Most workers in the construction industry start their careers as trainees or apprentices. Right now about 150,000 young people, between the ages of seventeen and twenty-seven, are learning their skills from older, experienced workers, called journeymen.

Many fine apprentice programs are run by the building trade unions. The programs for skilled workers take between two and five years, but training for laborers usually lasts only one to three months. Young apprentices learn by working alongside the journeymen and by attending school one or two nights a week. At first, they earn about half the salary of the journeymen. Every six months, though, they receive a raise. By the end of the program, they are earning almost a full journeyman's salary. When they complete the program, they are qualified journeymen.

The people working in building construction earn rather high salaries. Few other trades pay as much for workers without college degrees. The work is interesting and varied. No two projects are ever exactly the same.

Above: Apprentices learn by working alongside skilled workers.
Left: Apprentices also learn by attending school one or two nights a week.

There are opportunities throughout the country, in private and public industry, at home and abroad.

But there are certain risks too. The work in construction is often hard and dangerous. Since much of the work is out of doors, the workers are on the job in extreme heat and extreme cold and during rain and snow. When the weather gets very bad work stops, but so does the worker's salary.

There are other problems too. Most construction workers are hired by the job rather than by the week or month. When few buildings are under construction, they are laid off. They may be out of work for long stretches of time. Also, the construction industry has not offered many opportunities to women and minority workers. Only in the last few years has this industry slowly begun to accept them in apprenticeship programs and to hire them as skilled workers.

Nevertheless, the skilled workers in the building industry ply their trade with pride and distinction. The planners, the structural workers, the finish workers, and the mechanical workers are all part of a long tradition that started in ancient times, when the earliest construction workers piled up tree branches to build the very first house.

THE PLANNERS

Almost every construction project begins with the question, "Can you design a building for me?"

This question may be asked by a family that wants a new home; a business person that wants a store, factory, hotel or theater; a government agency that wants a new school or hospital; a religious group that wants a church or synagogue; or any other person or group of people that wishes a building for any purpose at all.

ARCHITECTS

This question is usually asked of an architect. Architects plan and design buildings. Their work is the important first step of the construction process.

All architects-to-be attend college. They study both the art and the science of designing buildings. The artistic side of architecture is concerned with the appearance of a building. The science of architecture is knowing how to erect safe, long-lasting buildings.

After earning their college degrees, the graduate architects spend a period of time working in the offices of experienced architects. Then they take the state examination for a license to go off on their own.

The people who ask the architects to design beautiful and useful buildings for them are called clients. Architects ask many questions to find out exactly what kinds of buildings the clients want. After that they go to their drawing boards, where they bring together their own artistic knowledge and visions with the clients' practical ideas and needs.

The architects set down their ideas in what are called line drawings. Some of the drawings, called elevations, show the various sides of the buildings, as seen from the outside. Other drawings, the floor plans, show the location, size, and arrangement of the rooms.

The architects present the line drawings or plans to the clients. The prospective owners may say, "I'd like a slightly larger kitchen," or, "Instead of small separate windows, I'd prefer one large picture window," or, "Must there be a post in the middle of the basement?" The architects discuss the plans with the clients. They point out any problems in carrying out the clients' wishes. They explain possible violations of zoning laws and building codes. They talk about costs.

Often, architects prepare a second set of line drawings. Again, they discuss them with their clients. This back-and-forth dialogue may continue for some time, until the architects and the clients agree on a plan that satisfies them both as to appearance, use, and safety.

ENGINEERS

Once the clients and architects have arrived at final designs, especially for very large buildings, other workers in the architects' offices are called in. They are the engineers.

Although the architects are trained in methods and materials of construction, the engineers are the construction specialists. Architects design mostly for beauty; engineers design mostly for strength. On small jobs, such as single-family homes, the architect may do both. But in large construction projects it is up to the engineers to select the best materials for a building. Engineers decide exactly how wide the beams should be; whether to use brick or concrete, cast iron or nickel steel; what is a proper capacity for the furnace; what size should the air conditioner be; and so on.

The engineers are also college graduates, trained in how to apply science to day-to-day problems. The engineer takes the architect's plans and prepares detailed drawings. The drawings show the many structural, safety, and mechanical features of the new building.

The rough plans are now brought to the drafting department of the architectural firm. The draftspeople, or renderers, working here are trained to produce exact and precise plans, called detail drawings, or working drawings, from the incomplete drawings they receive. They

Above: Architects set their ideas down in elevations, showing the outside of the building, and floor plans, showing the arrangement of the rooms. Below: The men and women in the drafting department prepare accurate and careful plans that show every detail of the building.

make accurate and careful plans on large sheets of paper that show every detail of the building. These drawings, called blueprints, are used by the construction workers once the building gets under way. About twenty to thirty separate pages of plans are made for a medium-sized building. They show the elevations from all sides, the floor plans of the building, the location of the heating, plumbing, and electrical systems, as well as the exact location of the building on the construction site.

At the same time the blueprints are being prepared, the architects and the engineers are preparing the building's specifications, or specs, as they are called. The specs spell out in words the exact size and type of materials to be used, and exactly how they are to be assembled or installed.

The approved plans and specs are next turned over to a builder or building contractor. The contractor agrees to erect the building according to the plans and specs.

GENERAL CONTRACTOR

General contractors need several special skills in order to succeed. Above all, they must know the building industry. Most begin as workers in a building trade or in an architect's office. Once they are on their own, they must always keep up with the times, and they must stay informed on the newest materials and the latest methods of construction.

General contractors also need a good understanding of how to organize a business, and how to run it at a profit.

A good grasp of building laws and taxes is a big help since builders are continually involved with government rules and regulations. And builders must be able to estimate costs and hire workers who can do the best job in the shortest time at the least cost.

Some small general contractors have just a few workers who do everything from drawing up the plans to erecting the building. In large firms, though, the work of the general contractor is divided among a number of people who are experts in certain phases of building construction.

ESTIMATORS

Among the first workers the general contractor calls on are the estimators. These men and women, usually college trained, use the architect's plans and specs to figure out the cost of the project. They bring to their job a wide and up-to-date knowledge of building methods and materials, as well as a knowledge of labor costs. By performing mathematical calculations quickly and correctly, the estimators come up with accurate cost figures. Usually clients ask several contractors for estimates. Therefore, each contractor wants to submit a price that is high enough to make a profit, yet low enough to be the best estimate and to win the job.

PURCHASING AGENTS

Once the contracts are signed and the contractor gets the go-ahead, the purchasing agents swing into ac-

Above: Architects, engineers, and general contractors meet to go over the building specifications. Below: A large general contractor employs a number of workers who are experts in various phases of building construction.

tion. It is their job to order all the building supplies and equipment that are needed to complete the building.

First of all, the purchasing agents must know where to order the materials listed in the specs, and how to get the lowest possible prices. Then, they must be able to find satisfactory substitutions if some products are not available. And perhaps most important of all, they must be sure that the materials will be delivered on schedule. If the delivery is too early there are problems of storage, damage by the weather, and danger of thievery. If the delivery is too late, the entire production schedule may be held up until some step can be finished.

PROJECT SUPERINTENDENT

The project superintendent, or job superintendent, is the key person in charge of the construction of a building. This job calls for a great deal of experience in the building trades. Along with this, an ability to work well with people and get things done is a must.

The project superintendent receives a complete set of plans and specs from the architects' office. After studying them carefully, the superintendent works out an approach to the job. What kinds of workers are needed? When? With what tools? In what order? Are there any special problems with the job? The project superintendent is expected to handle any difficulties that arise on the job. Whether from the contractor's office or at the building site, the superintendent directs all construction.

In addition to the people who work directly on build-

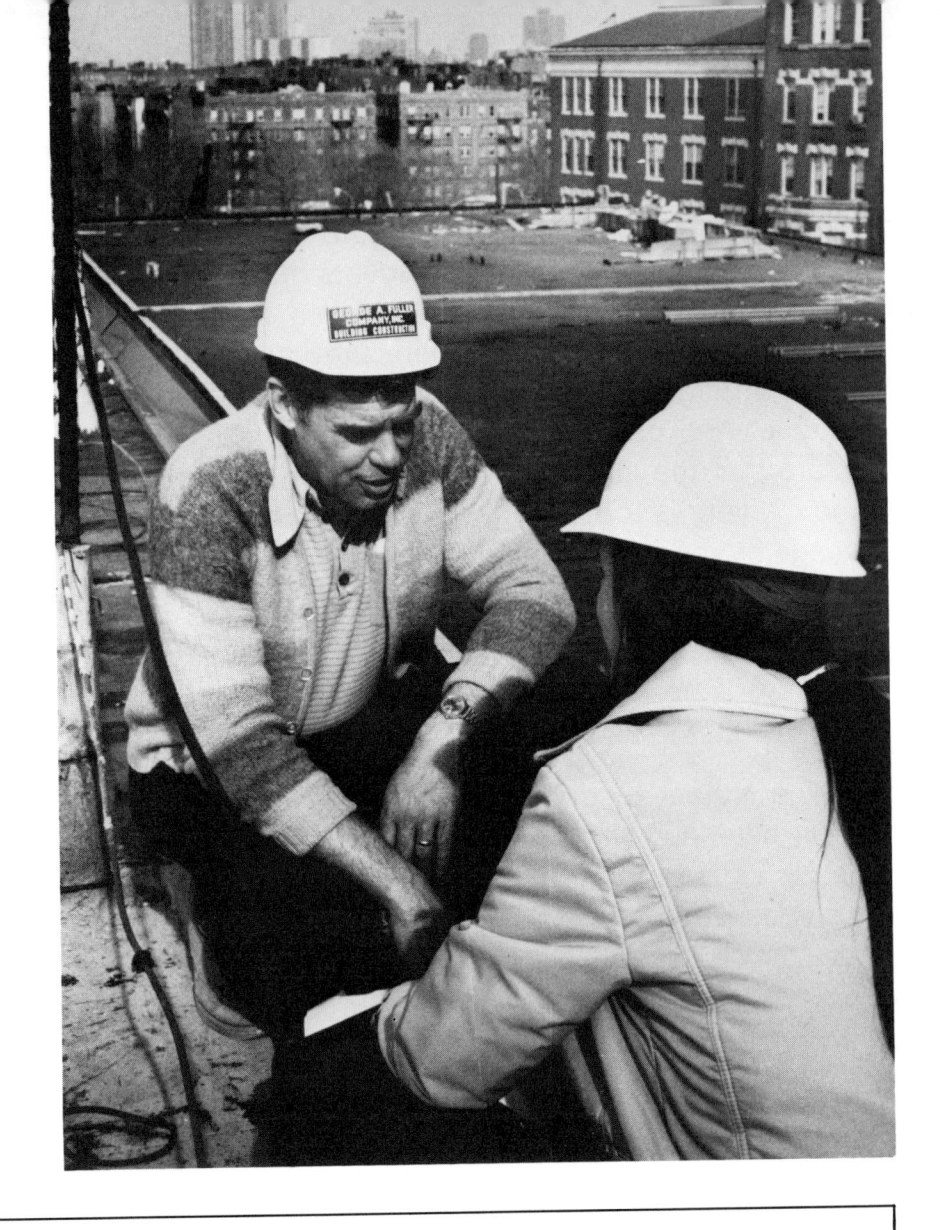

The project superintendent is the
person in charge of the building site.

ing projects, there are a good number of people in general contractors' offices who keep the company functioning. They range from salespeople, who bring clients to the construction company, to lawyers and accountants, who take care of the legal and financial affairs, to secretaries and clerks, who handle the paperwork.

In most building construction, the general contractor does only between 25 and 50 percent of the actual work. The rest is done by subcontractors, who specialize in certain building trades. Almost all general contractors will hire subcontractors to install heating and air-conditioning, electrical work, plumbing, and to do sheet metal and steel work. Most general contractors will also subcontract the roofing, painting, and plastering.

Planning is important to any project. But it is especially important in the building industry. The architects and engineers must plan every detail so that the finished building is exactly the one they envisioned. The general contractor must coordinate the entire construction schedule, from assembling the materials, to assigning the workers, to hiring the subcontractors, so that the job is started on time, progresses on schedule, and is completed by the promised date.

STRUCTURAL CRAFTS

The architect's and engineer's plans are now set. The general contractor and the subcontractors have been hired. The center of activity shifts to the building site.

SURVEYORS

The first workers to arrive at the building site are the surveyors. Usually there is one surveyor and two helpers. The helpers carry the transit, the main tool of the surveyors. The transit is a small telescope set on a three-legged stand. The surveyor uses it to measure the plot of land and to lay out the boundaries of the property and of the building.

The surveyor points the transit to a spot on the land, as shown on the architect's map, and looks through the eyepiece. The assistants hold up tall, thin, marked poles. The transit shows the exact distance to the poles and measures any rise or fall in the level of the land.

As the surveyor completes the measurements, the assistants knock wooden stakes into the ground. The stakes mark the boundary of the owner's site. They also put in stakes at the four corners of the building to outline the finished project.

EXCAVATORS

Excavators are earth movers. They are sometimes called operating engineers. They level and prepare the land for construction. They dig the deep holes that are needed for the foundations of most buildings. They clear the land of trees, bushes, and other obstacles.

One of the chief machines brought in to excavate land is the bulldozer, or "dozer," as it is always called. It is essentially a tractor with a large, sharp, slightly curved steel blade in front. The driver uses a power control to raise or lower the blade. The machine can scrape up a layer of dirt, uproot trees and bushes, or move boulders and rocks. The operators use the dozers to remove the top levels of soil as a first step in starting to dig a foundation. The excavators use the surveyor's stakes to guide them as they work with the dozer.

The front-end loader, or payloader, is one of the most popular digging machines. Like the dozer, it is built on a tractor. Its large, bucketlike shovel is mounted on the front of the tractor. The operators have controls to raise or lower the bucket. As they lower the bucket into the ground, the teeth along the bottom edge force their way into the soil or cut through the loose rock. When the bucket is full, the operators use the controls to raise and dump the load into a truck, which removes it from the site. Sometimes they pile the load on the ground to be used later.

The backhoe is another digging machine often used by excavators. The machine works like a garden hoe. The operators drop a sort of shovel, called a dipper, onto the ground. The dipper is then mechanically pulled forward. As it moves, it digs down and fills up with soil. Each dipper-full is either dumped into a truck or spread on the ground.

When putting up large, multistoried buildings, such as schools, hospitals, tall apartment houses, or office buildings, the excavation must be very deep and cover a great area. For these excavations, the workers use larger models of dozers, front-end loaders, and backhoes. They also use power, or dipper, shovels, which cut more deeply into the ground and remove greater amounts of soil and rock.

If the excavators need to dig into solid rock, they often blast with dynamite, TNT, or black powder. Drillers make holes in the rock, and specially trained workers place charges of explosives in the holes. When the explosives handlers set off the blast, the surrounding rock shatters. Then the operators use one of the powerful earth-moving machines to take away the debris.

CONCRETE WORKERS

Almost every house has a concrete foundation, which is made by concrete workers. The main purpose of the foundation is to support the structure above it. The founda-

Above: A worker guides the bulldozer operator as they clear the site for a building. Right: The carpenters and laborers have put the forms in place to hold the concrete for the building foundation.

tion spreads the weight of the house over a large area, making it more solid and secure. A house on a foundation is like a person on skis. If you stand on fresh snow, your feet sink into the snow. But with skis, your weight is distributed over a larger surface, and you tend to stay on top of the snow.

Most foundations for small houses are made from poured concrete. The workers in charge of laying the foundation are concrete workers, or masons. Carpenters and laborers work with them.

The carpenters are responsible for the wooden, moldlike forms into which the concrete is poured. Usually the contractors have a number of forms that they carry from job to job. Sometimes, though, the carpenters build new or different ones. They also build the braces that hold the forms in place.

The laborers do most of the work of assembling, locking, and bracing the forms in the excavation for the foundation. In addition, they prepare the walls of the forms to receive the concrete by spreading oil or water on the inside of the forms. This allows the concrete to dry better, and it makes it easier to remove the forms after the concrete is set.

Concrete is made of cement (a gray powder made from crushed stone) and aggregates (a mixture of sand and gravel). When water is mixed with dry cement and aggregates it becomes a thick paste, which can be poured for up to about an hour and a half before it hardens. The concrete is usually brought to the site in large mixing trucks. The cement, aggregates, and water combine in the slowly revolving chambers of the concrete mixers as the trucks are driven to the construction site.

At the site, the truck driver backs the concrete mixer up to the wooden or metal forms set in the ground. The laborers guide the concrete through a chute from the truck into the forms. They use large rakelike tools to spread it about.

The concrete pouring is done under the watchful eyes of the concrete masons. They make sure that the concrete is of the right thickness, that it is flowing well, and that the forms are holding the great weight of the concrete. After it is poured, the concrete masons move along the foundation wall, using flat trowels to smooth and level the top surface. They work quickly to shape the material before it sets and hardens.

Sometimes the concrete masons set heavy metal rods into the forms. The rods are buried inside the concrete. This makes reinforced concrete, which is stronger and better able to support the weight of larger buildings.

For some tall buildings, the architect's plans may call for concrete columns, or piers, to carry the structure. Then the carpenters prepare forms for upright columns, instead of for the usual foundation walls. At the bottom of the column they build forms for big, flat slabs of concrete, called footings, to spread out the weight of the column over a greater area. The masons put metal rods inside the wooden forms to reinforce the column. The concrete is poured from above, often by means of a bucket which is tilted over the top of the forms.

It may take a few days for the concrete to harden and

Above: The concrete mixer is driven to the building site, and the concrete is poured for the foundation. Left: Sometimes the cement masons have the concrete poured around heavy metal rods, which make the foundation walls stronger.

dry completely. Often, laborers will spray water on the concrete each day to keep it slightly moist. Moist concrete hardens more slowly, but it hardens better. As soon as the concrete is dry, the concrete masons direct the laborers to strip away the forms. The foundation is finished.

If the foundation is for a small house, carpenters come in and start to frame in the rest of the house. For other buildings, from large houses to skyscrapers, a crew of ironworkers is required to put the steel for the structure into place.

IRONWORKERS

Plans for a very large house often call for ironworkers to install one or more large steel beams across the length of the house. First, the ironworkers usually set up some Lally columns. These are steel posts that are sometimes filled with concrete. The workers rest or bolt the beam into place on the posts. Later, the boards that support the floor are laid across the beam.

In bigger, taller buildings, the plans show the ironworkers where to install the many steel columns, girders, and beams that make up the framework of the building. A skyscraper, for example, is basically an all-steel structure. The walls and floors are placed on, or hung from, the steel structure.

The site of a skyscraper is excavated down to a solid layer of bedrock. Wooden forms are set on the bedrock. Concrete is poured into the forms to create huge footings.

On top of each footing, the ironworkers set a structure made of crossed steel beams, called a grillage. A typical grillage weighs about forty tons. They make sure that the massive grillage is perfectly centered and perfectly level on the footing. Construction workers then force concrete through the openings and between the beams of the grillage, and they bury the entire structure in concrete.

Extending up from the center of each grillage are several heavy steel plates. The ironworkers attach a steel column to these plates to support the structure. Each grillage, firmly set in concrete, holds its column solidly in place. The millions of pounds of superstructure rests securely on the grillages and the concrete footings.

The columns, girders, and beams arrive at the site with code numbers that tell exactly where each piece should be placed. The columns are the up and down, or vertical, supports. The girders run from column to column. The beams connect the girders. The girders and beams support the weight of the floors. Together with the columns, they form the skeleton of the skyscraper.

Once the columns are in place, operating engineers use cranes to hoist the steel girders up into place. Ironworkers clamber up the columns and use long tapered metal rods, called drift pins, to attach the girder to the columns. When both ends of the girder are in place, the workers secure them with temporary bolts. Still later, when the columns and girders are lined up perfectly, they bolt, weld, or rivet them together permanently.

The ironworkers next attach the beams to the girders. Once the beams are in place, laborers place wooden

The crane operator raises the heavy
steel to the level where it is needed.

planks across them, making a temporary floor. This floor is a much safer working surface than the narrow beams and girders. It also protects the workers below from any falling building materials, and it provides a base for working on the next floor.

Many people think that the ironworkers who specialize in the "high steel" of skyscrapers have the most glamorous jobs in the building industry. Indeed, it is exciting to walk and work on narrow steel ledges, hundreds of feet above the ground. But it is very dangerous as well. The work is strenuous, and at these heights it causes many accidents. In addition to the stress of difficult work under trying conditions, ironworkers also have to contend with rain and snow and extremes of temperature.

ROUGH CARPENTERS

Once the structural concrete and ironwork is done on almost any building, the carpenters get ready to do their work. Dressed in overalls, and usually carrying hammers, nails, saws, and other tools, their job is to take care of all the woodworking tasks.

There are two kinds of carpenters: rough carpenters and finish carpenters. Rough carpenters do necessary work that may later be covered up and not be seen in the completed building. The finish carpenters do the finer work that will show. Rough carpenters build the frames for the concrete foundation. They also build the scaffolds that are used to reach the parts of the house above the ground level and construct any temporary toolsheds or offices that are needed at the site. And they build the frames and supports for the floors, walls, and ceilings of the house.

But now the rough carpenters get ready to put in the floor joists. The joists support the subflooring and the flooring, as well as all the loads placed on the floors. They are heavy beams, usually 2 inches (5.08 cm) thick, and anywhere from 6 to 12 inches (15.24 to 30.48 cm) long. The carpenters install them to run across the area of the house, usually with the centers of each beam 16 inches (40.64 cm) apart.

The rough carpenters then lay large sheets of plywood, called the subfloor, on top of the floor joists. The plywood usually comes in large 4-foot (1.2 m) by 8-foot (2.4 m) panels. The carpenters use large nails and heavy hammers to attach the subflooring to the joists. They use small, electrical, circular saws to cut down any panels that are too large, and that extend beyond the size of the floor. Whenever possible, they try to use the leftover pieces. Good carpenters waste very little wood.

The subflooring can serve as a platform for the carpenters to assemble the frames for the walls of the house. They use long planks of 2-by-4-inch (5 by 10 cm) lumber for the frames. One 2-by-4 becomes the lower, horizontal plate. Every 16 inches (40.64 cm), an 8-foot (2.4 m) long 2-by-4, called a stud, is nailed to the lower plate. Two 2-by-4s, nailed across the top, become the top of the wall.

Some carpenters build the frames of the walls on the subfloor, and then they tilt and raise them into place. Others prefer to build the frames directly where they will be

Above: Much of the rough carpenters' work is later covered and not seen in the finished building. Right: The rough carpenters use planks of 2-by-4 lumber to build the frames for the walls of the house.

standing. With both methods, after the framing for each wall is done, a line of big nails, each one driven in by a few powerful hammer blows, secures the frame to the flooring and the foundation of the house.

The line of vertical studs is interrupted at the places where there will be windows or doors in the wall. Here the carpenters saw through the studs and build special frames to support the studs, despite the cuts for the openings.

The rough carpenters nail the ceiling joists across the top of the wall frames. They are similar in size and spacing to the floor joists. They will support the weight of the ceiling and any load placed on the attic floor.

The carpenters nail another set of similar beams, called rafters, to the ceiling joists. They form the usual pitched or angled roof of the house. Their size is specified by the engineer, based on the weight of the roof, as well as the weight of the maximum amount of snow that can be expected for the area.

The joists, studs, and rafters are the frame, or skeleton, of the house. Once they are complete, the carpenters sheath the frame, or put a skin over the skeleton. They nail 4-by-8-foot (1.2 by 2.4 m) plywood panels all over the outside of the walls and the top of the roof rafters. As with the subfloor, they must saw off sections of some panels to make a perfect fit.

The installation of the wall and roof sheathing is an important moment in the construction of a building. It marks the completion of the structural work. The basic building is built.

But the building is still far from ready to be turned over to the new owners. All the rough work must be covered over or finished. Many details, some big, some small, must be added. And all of the building's mechanical systems, such as electricity, water, and heat, must be put into operation.

FINISHING CRAFTS

The first crew to start working on the completed basic building are the so-called finish workers. Their job is to install weatherproof roof and wall coverings all over the outside of the building. Inside, they put up the walls, floors, and stairs, and add dozens of items, such as insulation, closets, cabinets, and shelves. And finally, they decorate the building with either paint or wallpaper or both.

ROOFERS

Roofers are specialists who almost always work for separate roofing subcontractors rather than for general contractors. When they arrive on the scene, the house usually has just a plywood underroof. The roofers follow the architect's plans, which show what materials to apply to the roof as protection against all possible weather conditions. In cold, snowy climates, the roofs tend to be made of more sturdy materials than roofs in drier, warmer climates.

Roofers use steep ladders or scaffolding to climb up to the roofs. They carry with them heavy hammers, chisels, knives, and shears, as well as apron pockets full of roofer's nails. The first time up, they also bring rolls of specially treated roofing paper.

The roofers unroll the paper and nail it into place on the plywood underroof. When they come to the edge of the roof, they cut the paper off with a sharp, stubby knife. Then they start back again, covering another wide section from one end of the roof to the other. Back and forth they go until they have nailed a layer of heavy black paper over the entire wood-sheathed roof. The paper is a waterproof base for the roof.

The top covering of the roof is usually some kind of shingle. Shingles are either thin pieces of wood, asphalt, asbestos, slate, or tile. Asphalt shingles are most often used in homes that are built in moderate climates.

The roofers carry piles of these shingles up to the roof. They nail them in place in rows starting at one bottom corner of the sloping roof, and they work their way across to the bottom corner on the opposite side. Then, they nail down another row, overlapping the first row with the second. With their powerful shears or knives, they cut out the shingles as they go around pipes and chimneys. They continue nailing the shingles in rows until the entire roof is shingled.

Most houses have sloping roofs to drain off the heavy

Above: Roofers usually work for separate subcontractors. They nail roofing paper and shingles into place on the underroof. Left: This student is learning how to nail roof shingles in straight lines as part of a high school course in building construction. Right: To make a built-up roof, the roofers spread hot, melted tar and asphalt between levels of tar paper.

rains or snow. Many large buildings, though, have flat roofs, which use pipes to carry away the water. Here the roofers make built-up roofs. They nail several layers of tar paper or roofing felt to the wood sheathing. Between each layer they apply a coat of hot, melted tar and asphalt to make a tight, waterproof seal over the entire roof. The final cover may be a heavy tar coating spread with a layer of fine gravel.

OUTSIDE FINISH CARPENTERS

There are many different materials that can be used as siding to cover the outside walls of buildings. The most common are wood, brick, stone, stucco, concrete, or aluminum. Usually the general contractors hire subcontractors to install the siding.

First, finish carpenters who work outside of the building nail heavy treated sheathing paper to the plywood sheathing. This is similar to the way paper is spread on the underroof. The paper covers all the outside walls of the building, making them waterproof. The carpenters work with particular care around the doors and windows to be sure that no water, wind, or dust is able to pass through. The siding will be placed directly over the tar paper.

The siding is often of wood. The simplest sidings are the several kinds of special plywoods that are made to be used for exterior siding. There are also wooden shingles and clapboards. Carpenters install them the way roofers attach shingles to the roof. The carpenters nail the first row, called a course, across the bottom of the wall. They overlap the second course over the first one as they nail it into place. They add course after course until they reach the top of the wall.

BRICKLAYERS

Bricklayers build two kinds of brick walls. They can build the walls entirely of brick, or they can cement the bricks into place as the outer surface of a wooden wall.

To lay up a brick wall, bricklayers start at the corners of the building. They lay the bricks on their flat sides in a horizontal layer, or course. The bricklayers use a tight string stretched across the wall, called a mason's line, to check that the course is straight. With a trowel, the bricklayers spread a layer of mortar between the bricks. (Mortar is like concrete, but without the coarse aggregate.) They place each brick on the mortar and tap it into place. They cut bricks with a mason's hammer to fit around windows and to complete rows.

Bricklayers arrange the bricks in various designs, called bonds. The bonds are staggered and this overlap makes the wall strong. The mortar between the bricks holds the bricks in place and makes the wall watertight.

Bricklayers are among the highest paid workers in the construction industry. They are assisted by unskilled workers who deliver the bricks and cement to the bricklayer.

Bricklayers work mostly out of doors, often while standing on scaffolds. Their work involves a lot of bend-

Above: Students spread heavy, treated paper over the plywood sheathing to make the outside walls waterproof. Right: Bricklayers sometimes build walls out of cinder blocks, instead of bricks.

ing, stooping, and lifting. They do not spend too much time on any one job. Mostly they move from job to job.

STONE MASONS AND CONCRETE MASONS

The stone masons either build solid stone walls, or more commonly, cover wood sheathing with a layer of veneer stone. Sometimes just the lower section of a building wall is covered with stone. Other materials are used for the upper sections.

Masons place the stones according to the builder's plans. They use mallets and crowbars to move the heavy stones into position. They use string with a weight at the end, called a plumb line, to keep the stones straight and even. They chip away with a mason's hammer or split and saw the stones that must be trimmed to fit in place. And they use mortar to cement the stones in place.

When the plans call for concrete or stucco walls, the concrete masons are called in. They spread the concrete on the wall either by hand or by blowing it through a hose. Then they give it the desired texture—smooth, rough, pebbly, or whatever—with trowels and other finishing tools.

INTERIOR FINISH CARPENTERS

While the outside workers are enclosing the house, other workers are adding insulation, constructing inside walls, installing floors, and hanging doors and windows.

Insulation is installed in the unfinished walls and ceiling. The insulation traps a layer of air in place. Still air is an excellent barrier to the flow of heat. During the winter it prevents heat from escaping; during the summer it prevents the heat of the sun from entering the building. Insulation makes the house more comfortable year round. It also makes it cheaper to run. With insulation, less fuel is burned during the winter to heat the house, and less energy is used during the summer to cool it.

Several insulating materials are used in new home construction. They come in different forms. Loose or foam insulation can be blown into the walls and ceilings by insulation subcontractors. Insulation also comes in rolls, wrapped in long strips of paper. The insulation workers install this type by nailing or stapling it to the wall studs or ceiling joists.

Carpenters build inside walls to form rooms. One of the most popular interior wall materials that they use is called drywall or Sheetrock. The carpenters nail these panels of paper-covered plaster directly to the studs. Later, painters will cover the nail heads and the joints between the panels with paper tape and plaster, in an operation called spackling. This makes smooth surfaces for painting or papering.

Drywall started as a cheap substitute for walls of plaster, a type of cement used for inside work. Now it has largely replaced plaster in home building. In commercial building, though, plaster walls are still widely used.

Before making a plaster wall, workers, called lathers,

Above: The worker wears a mask for protection as he sprays foam insulation in a steel building. Right: The interior finish carpenter measures carefully as he gets ready to install a wall.

nail a metal mesh, the lath, to the studs. Then plasterers apply the first coat of plaster on top of the lath base. They apply the plaster with enough force to push some through the openings of the lath, which adds strength.

Then the plasterers smooth the surface of the plaster. They make sure that it is straight and true. Just before it dries, they use a rakelike tool to make a crisscross of scratches on the surface. This roughness makes a better bond for the second coat of plaster, which they then apply.

The plasterers take great care with the surface of the second coat. They get it as smooth and straight as possible before applying the third and final coat. The last coat is very thin. The plasterers work quickly with trowels, brushes, and water to get it absolutely flat.

The third popular interior wall covering is wooden or plastic paneling. The paneling comes in large sheets, and the carpenters nail them to the studs. They often use nails with colored heads that are invisible against the colored paneling.

At some time during the finishing work, depending on the particular job, the carpenters install the windows and doors. Most windows arrive from the lumberyard with the glass in place and cut to size. Carpenters install them in the spaces that were left in the frame. Doors and door frames are also usually bought ready-made. The carpenters set them in the proper positions. To get a perfect fit, though, the carpenters almost always have to trim and adjust the frame, the window, or the door. This is exacting work. It requires great care and attention to detail.

PAINTERS AND PAPERHANGERS

With the exception of the paneling, every surface in the house is either painted or covered with wallpaper. The workers who do this are painters and paperhangers. Sometimes the same people do both jobs. Usually, though, they specialize in one trade or the other.

It may seem that painting is one of the simplest of the building trades. But this is not so. Skilled painters must know a great deal about their craft.

Painters first prepare the various surfaces for painting. They sandpaper or scrape any rough spots and fill in any cracks, holes, or knots in the woodwork. They then prepare the paints. This includes knowing which paints to use for the different areas, and how to mix paints to get the exact colors the clients want. Then, using a brush, roller, or spray gun, they apply the first coat of paint. The first coat is usually either a primer or a sealer coat. After this coat has completely dried, they apply one or two finish coats.

Paperhangers cover the walls, ceilings, and woodwork of rooms with wallpaper. They, too, must prepare the surfaces before hanging the paper. Sometimes they spread a coat of sizing, a gluelike liquid, to seal the surface and make it sticky enough to receive the paper.

Paperhangers then measure the space that is to be covered. They compute how much paper is needed, and they cut lengths of paper from long rolls, being sure to match the pattern from strip to strip. With a wide brush, they spread paste all over the back of the wallpaper and

Painters work both inside and outside the building.

press it firmly against the wall. By hand and with a smoothing brush, they smooth it into position, getting rid of all wrinkles and creases.

While the finishing workers are doing their jobs on the building, another group of workers is also doing various tasks around the building. These are the mechanical workers. They are the ones who actually make the building "work."

MECHANICAL CRAFTS

Each of the mechanical craft workers, the plumbers, electricians, heating and air-conditioning installers, and elevator constructors, work at the building site at various times during the structural and finishing stages of construction.

They fit their schedule to the progress that is made on the building. For some construction jobs, certain pipes have to be in place before the concrete is poured. There are many pipes, as well as wires, ducts, and other systems, that are most easily installed before the walls are nailed on. Yet most of the fixtures, appliances, lights, and other equipment cannot be put into place until the building is nearly finished.

Mechanical craft workers are among the most highly trained and skilled workers in the building trades. Before they can get a license to work, they usually must pass a test given by a state or local government agency. The test is on their knowledge of the trade, and their ability to practice it safely and properly.

PLUMBERS

The plumbers provide the new building with some pipes that bring in gas and water and other pipes that carry out waste water, or sewage. They also install and connect bathroom, kitchen, and laundry fixtures and other equipment throughout the building.

The plumbing contractor receives a set of plans from the architect. The plans show where the plumbing fixtures are to be located in the building. The specs describe the size and quality of the fixtures and pipes to be used. The plumbing contractors usually draw up their own plans showing exactly how they will run the pipes to each plumbing fixture in the building.

The water for most buildings in or near cities comes from a water main. The water main is a large underground pipe that brings the water from a central pumping station. To get the water, each individual building must be connected to the water main. Houses out in the country have to have a well dug for their water.

When the building's foundation is being laid, either the contractor or the water supply company digs a narrow trench from the water main to the building. The plumbers put lengths of pipe in the trench and join them to make one long pipe. They connect one end to the main;

they bring the other end up to the building. Once the pipe is hooked up, they cover it over with dirt, burying it beneath the surface.

At the same time, the plumbers lay a plastic or cast iron waste water pipe, which runs from the house to the city sewage system. In areas where there are no sewers, the wastes flow into a cesspool or septic tank buried near the house. The water from the tank flows into the ground; the sludge remains in the tank until it dissolves. Eventually the tank has to be cleaned and treated.

Most of the water pipes inside the building are hidden within the walls or beneath the floors of the building. Plumbers do most of this work, called "roughing in," beginning when the carpenters frame the building and ending when they close up the walls, floors, and ceilings. Timing is very important here. The superintendent makes sure that the pipes are delivered to the building site, and the plumbers are ready to start work before the carpenters finish the framing. Any delay in roughing in the plumbing can add considerable time and expense to the construction of the house.

Plumbers use power machines to cut, thread, and bend lengths of pipe that will bring the water to the kitchen, bathroom, laundry room, and furnace room. They make the joints watertight with melted lead and solder. These lines must be installed with great care. Leaking pipes can damage walls and furnishings. Repairs are difficult since they involve breaking through the walls to reach the pipes.

Besides the pipes that bring clean water to each part

Student plumbers sharpen their skills in contests run by the Vocational Industrial Clubs of America.

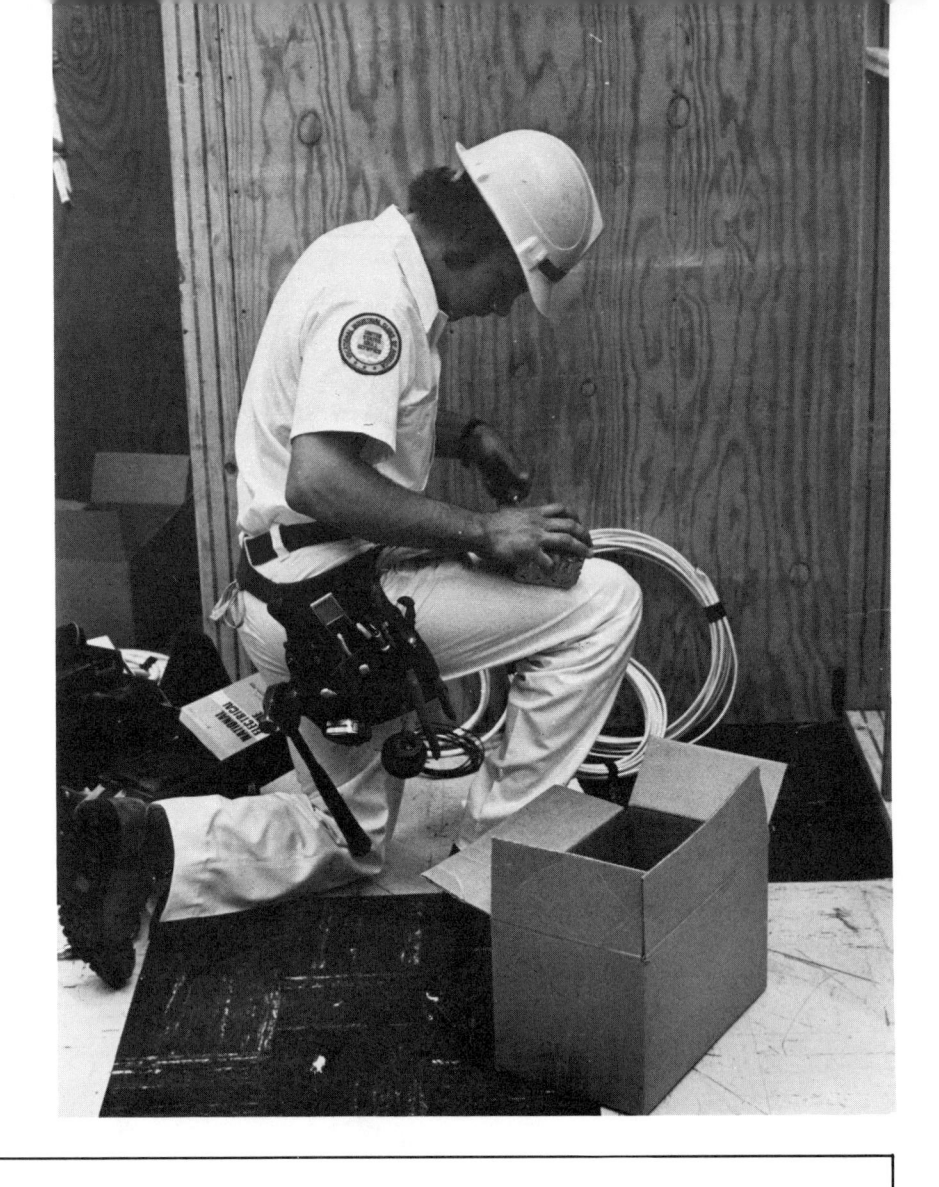

Wearing his tools around his waist, the young electrician installs the wiring in the walls of the house.

of the building, plumbers also install pipes to carry waste water away. All of the individual collecting pipes are hooked up to a single pipe that carries the wastes out to a sewer line or cesspool.

As soon as the "roughing in" is done, the plumbers leave the construction site to work elsewhere. They do not return until the other building trade workers have completed their jobs. Then it is time for them to do the finish work, installing the plumbing fixtures.

Now the plumbers unpack their small hand tools, such as wrenches, metal saws, pliers, and others. They cut short lengths of pipe to fit through the walls. They connect all the various sinks, tubs, showers, faucets, and washing machines to the pipes already hidden in the walls and floors. They adjust and test them until they are in perfect working order.

Plumbing, one of the most highly skilled trades, is well paid and the work is fairly steady. When the plumbers are not working on new construction, they do repairs and maintenance work in older buildings.

ELECTRICIANS

Just as plumbers bring a flow of water into a building, so electricians bring in a flow of electricity. They connect the wires that carry the electricity, and they hook up all the lights and other electrical fixtures.

The electrical contractors, too, are given the builder's plans, which show the location of the electrical fixtures and the type of wire that is required. It is up to the electricians, though, to plan the wiring system so that there will be a sufficient and safe flow of electricity.

The electricians get the electricity from an outside service line. This line is either on tall poles or buried. Usually electricians who work for the electric company run a wire from the service line to the house.

The electricians do their roughing in right after the carpenters have framed the house. Following the blueprints and the specs, they connect the wire bringing in the electricity to a panel of circuit breakers, or fuses. This is a safety device. If too much current is flowing or if there is a short circuit, the circuit breaker, or fuse, automatically cuts off the electricity.

From the panel, the electricians lay conduits. Conduits are flexible hollow pipes that protect the wires. The electricians bend and saw the conduits so that they are the right shapes and lengths. They drill holes through the studs and joists to carry the conduits through the walls, floors, and ceilings to every room in the building. Then they thread insulated wires from the panel through the conduits to all the outlets, lights, switches, and motors. Sometimes they have to pull the conduits and wires through some very tight places. They join the wires by splicing or by using special fasteners.

Electricians are done with the roughing in before the finish workers are too far along with their work. They leave for other jobs, and return only after the finishing is done. Then they install and connect the wires, which are now hidden in the walls, to the various electric switches and outlets around the building. They also connect different types of lighting fixtures in each room.

Even though a building inspector will go over the wiring, the electricians check and test every electrical circuit. They use electric test meters and other means to be sure that each one is connected properly and working safely. Electricians, more than any other construction workers, treat electricity with a good deal of fear and respect. They know how dangerous it can be.

HEATING AND AIR-CONDITIONING INSTALLERS

The heating and air-conditioning workers install, connect, and adjust both the heating and the air-conditioning systems in new buildings.

At the heart of most heating systems is a furnace. Almost every furnace produces heat by burning fuel oil. The heat is usually transferred to the rest of the building in one of three ways: water is heated and circulated; water is heated to make steam, and the steam is circulated; or air is heated and circulated.

The heating installers follow the architect's plans and specs as to the type of heating unit and its placement. They also follow the directions for locating the oil tank and the radiators or hot air outlets in each room. It is up to them, though, to decide how to carry the hot steam, water, or hot air to the rest of the building, and how to run the fuel lines that feed oil to the furnace.

The heating experts often call on plumbers to prepare pipes for the hot water and the steam heating systems. They call on sheet metal workers to prepare the metal ducts to carry the hot air to the rooms. In these cases, though, the heating experts still direct and supervise the other workers.

Up until recently, heating specialists mostly installed oil-burning furnaces. Now, though, more and more buildings are being heated by solar energy. Many heating installers are learning how to build and install solar heating systems.

Air-conditioning specialists seldom install individual air conditioners. They mostly set up central air-conditioning systems that cool off entire buildings.

When they install central air conditioners, the workers either follow an architect's plans, or they use their own judgment in placing the large main unit and hooking it up to a source of electricity. Often, they enlist the help of sheet metal workers to build ducts that will carry the cold air to the separate rooms.

After the duct work and electrical connections are done, the air-conditioning installers are responsible for starting up the system and checking it out, even in the cold of winter. While it can be pleasant testing air conditioners in the summer, it can be extremely uncomfortable in the winter.

ELEVATOR CONSTRUCTORS

Elevator constructors almost never work on small houses; but these skilled workers make very tall buildings

Special workers install the heating systems, such as this large unit in a hospital.

possible. They assemble and install elevators, which carry both people and goods to all the floors of multi-storied buildings and skyscrapers. While most of the other mechanical craft workers are hired by subcontractors, most elevator constructors work for elevator manufacturers.

When a building is to have an elevator, the plans leave room for the elevator shaft, for the machinery to run the elevator, and for the doors to enter the elevator on every floor.

The first step in installing an elevator is for the workers to attach guide rails. These rails run up and down the entire height of a building, inside the elevator shaft, and control the movement of the elevator.

The workers next put the hoisting machinery into place. This is usually done at the top of the elevator shaft, high above the top floor of the building. Very often, the workers must use wrenches, pliers, power saws, and drills in tiny, cramped spaces, with barely enough room for themselves besides the massive machinery.

The final step is to assemble the passenger car itself and attach it to the heavy steel cables, which carry it up and down. The workers also add the safety devices that prevent the car from falling to the bottom of the shaft in case of an accident to the cables or controls.

Skilled elevator constructors must be capable of doing the mechanical work on the elevator without any sloppiness or error. They must also have a good understanding of the principles of electricity and electronics.

In a busy building, hundreds of people depend on the elevators they build every day.

CONCLUSION

Various building trade workers are usually working side by side as the building nears completion. There are carpenters and electricians, bricklayers and iron workers, plumbers and steam fitters, plasterers, painters, and paperhangers. When they are all finished, the building is about ready to be turned over to the owners.

The only job that remains is the clean-up. Scraps of wood and metal, sections of ducts, wiring, and pipes, paint cans and paper scraps, as well as coffee cups and lunch wrappers, are littered over the house and grounds. The general contractor usually sends in a team of laborers to clean up the building and its site. The laborers collect and cart away all the trash in trucks. They also go over the entire building, washing the windows, waxing the floors, removing the protective wrapping from the appliances, and in general preparing the building for the people who will be moving in.

The very last job is usually landscaping the grounds around the building. Subcontractors who do landscape gardening level the land, and they plant grass, shrubs, flowers and trees. The gardeners often work together as a crew. Within a day or two they are able to change the raw dirt and rocks of a busy construction site into an attractive lawn and garden.

By the time the family moves into the new house, the construction workers are already at another construction site.

During the construction period, the client, the architect, and the general contractor visit the site many times. Sometimes one or the other asks for some small changes. Whenever possible these are made.

Now they come out for the final visit. This time the contractor turns over a set of keys to the client, who many months earlier first asked the architect to design a building. With great pride and great anticipation, the owners enter their new building. The construction workers who made it all possible are nowhere to be seen. They are already at work elsewhere, meeting the challenge of still another building project.

FURTHER READING

General books on the construction industry:

Grow, Thomas A. *Construction: A Guide to the Profession.* Englewood Cliffs, N.J.: Prentice-Hall, 1975.
Steinberg, Joseph, and Stempel, Martin. *Practices and Methods of Construction.* Englewood Cliffs, N.J.: Prentice-Hall, 1957.

Career books on building construction:

Daly, Donald F. *Aim for a Job in Building Trade.* New York: Richard Rosen, 1970.
Liebers, Arthur. *Jobs in Construction.* New York: Lothrop, Lee & Shepard, 1973.
Spence, W. *Construction: Industry and Careers.* Englewood Cliffs, N.J.: Prentice-Hall, 1976.

The following organizations have printed material available on various phases of building construction:

Bureau of Apprenticeship and Training
Department of Labor
Washington, D.C. 20210
(Ask for *Jobs for Which Apprenticeships are Available,* and other pamphlets.)

General Building Contractors Association, Inc.
36 South 18th Street
Philadelphia, PA. 19103
(Ask for *Construction: Building Your Future.*)

National Association of Home Builders
15th & M Streets, N.W.
Washington, D.C. 20005
(Ask for *Build a Better Life.*)

Vocational Industrial Clubs of America
105 N. Virginia Avenue
Falls Church, Virginia 22046
(A national organization for trade students; write for information.)

INDEX

Air conditioning, 7, 48, 55–56
Architects, 4, 10–12, 15, 19, 20, 25, 35, 49, 55, 56, 61
Architecture, 10, 11, 12

Backhoe, 22
Beams, 27, 28, 30, 31, 33
Blueprints, 14, 54
Bricklayers, 4, 39–41, 59
Building codes, 11, 14
Bulldozers, 21, 22

Carpenters, 4, 7, 9, 24, 25, 27, 30–47, 50, 54, 59
Ceilings, 50, 54
Cesspool, 50, 53
Clients, 11, 12, 19, 61
Concrete, 24, 25, 27, 28, 41, 48
Concrete mixers, 25
Conduits, 54
Construction, 1, 7, 9, 17, 21
    building, 1, 15, 19
    heavy, 1

industry, 14
materials, 12, 14, 15, 17
methods, 2, 4, 11, 12, 14, 15
process, 10
project, 4, 10, 15, 19, 21
Contractors, 4, 14–15, 19, 20, 24, 35, 38, 49, 59, 61

Dipper shovels. *See* Power shovels
Dozers. *See* Bulldozers
Drawings, 11, 12
Drywall, 42

Electricians, 7, 48, 53–55, 59
Elevations, 11, 14, 58
Engineers, 4, 12–14, 19, 20, 21, 22, 28, 33

Floor plans, 11, 14
Floors, 30, 31, 33, 35, 41, 50, 54
Footings, 25, 27, 28
Foundations, 21, 22, 24, 27, 33, 49
Framing, 50

[64]

Front-end loader. *See* Payloader
Furnace, 55

Girders, 27, 28, 30
Grillage, 27, 28

Heating installers, 48, 55–56

Insulation, 42
Ironworkers, 4, 27–30, 59

Joists, 31, 33, 42, 54

Lally columns, 27, 28

Masons, 4, 22, 24, 25, 41
Minority workers, 9
Mortar, 39, 41

Painters, 4, 42, 45–47, 59
Paperhangers, 45–47, 59
Payloader, 21, 22
Piers, 25
Pipes, 49, 56
    gas, 49
    sewage, 49
    waste water, 49, 50, 53
    water, 49, 50
Planners, 4, 7, 9, 10–19
Plasterers, 4, 44, 59
Plumbers, 7, 48, 49–53, 55, 59
Power shovels, 22

Project superintendent. *See* Superintendent

Rafters, 33
Roof, 35–38

Salary, 7, 9
Septic tank. *See* Cesspool
Sheathing, 33, 38, 41
Shingles, 36
Siding, 38
Skyscraper, 27, 28, 30, 58
Spackling, 42
Specifications. *See* Specs
Specs, 14, 15, 17, 49, 54, 55
Studs, 31, 33, 42, 44, 54
Subcontractors, 19, 20
Superintendent, 17–19, 50

Transit, 20

Unions, 7

Walls, 31, 35, 38, 41, 42, 45, 50, 53, 54
    brick, 38
    concrete, 41
    drywall, 42
    paneling, 44, 45
    plaster, 42
    stone, 41
    stucco, 41
Women, 9

Zoning laws, 11

(See Career Index on next page)

CAREER INDEX

Accountants, 19
Air-conditioning installers, 7, 48, 55–56
Apprentices, 7
Architects, 4, 10–12, 15, 19, 20, 25, 35, 49, 55, 56, 61

Bricklayers, 4, 39–41, 59
Building inspector, 55

Carpenters, 4, 24, 25, 27, 50, 54, 59
    finish, 4, 7, 9, 30, 35–47, 54
    interior finish, 41–44
    outside finish, 38–39
    rough, 30–34
Cement workers, 4
Clerks, 19
Construction workers, 14, 15, 17, 28, 30, 39, 41, 42, 53, 55, 56, 58, 61
Contractors, 4, 14–15, 19, 20, 24, 35, 38, 49, 59, 61
    general, 59, 61

Draftspeople, 12
Drillers, 22

Electricians, 7, 48, 53–55, 59
Elevator constructors, 48, 56–59
Engineers, 4, 12–14, 19, 20, 33
    operating, 4, 21, 22, 28
Estimators, 15
Excavators, 21–22
Explosives handlers, 22

Gardeners, 59

Heating installers, 7, 48, 55–56
Helpers, 20

Insulation workers, 42
Ironworkers, 4, 27–30, 59

Journeymen, 7

Laborers, 4, 24, 27, 28, 59
Lathers, 42–44
Lawyers, 19

Marble setters, 4
Masons, 4, 22, 24, 25, 41
Mechanical craft workers, 7, 9, 48–61

Painters, 4, 42, 45–47, 59
Paperhangers, 45–47, 59
Planners, 4, 7, 9, 10–19
Plasterers, 4, 44, 59
Plumbers, 7, 48, 49–53, 55, 59
Purchasing agents, 15–17

Renderers, 12
Roofers, 4, 35–38

Salespeople, 19
Secretaries, 19
Sheet metal workers, 4, 56
Skilled workers, 7, 9, 48, 56
Steamfitters, 59
Structural crafts workers, 4, 9, 20–34
Subcontractors, 19, 20
Superintendent, 17–19, 50
Surveyors, 20–21

Tile setters, 4

Unskilled workers, 39

3 9123 00158839 6
HACKENSACK-JOHNSON LIBRARY

a39123001588396b

89

J690   327679
Berger
Building construction.

DATE DUE

Johnson Free Public Library
Hackensack, New Jersey